Twelve Chosen Men Who Changed the World

By Dr. Curtis Hutson

SWORD OF THE LORD PUBLISHERS
Murfreesboro, Tennessee

ISBN 0-87398-027-1

Printed in the U.S.A.

TABLE OF CONTENTS

The Apostles

SCRIPTURE READING:
Matthew 10:1-8; Mark 3:13-21; Luke 6:12-19; Acts 1:13

I. WHAT IS THE DIFFERENCE BETWEEN AN APOSTLE AND A DISCIPLE?

You have probably noticed in reading through the New Testament that sometimes the twelve were called disciples and sometimes they were called apostles. Before we begin a study of their individual lives, let us understand the difference between an apostle and a disciple.

A. DISCIPLE—A learner who seeks to imitate his teacher; in other words, a pupil, a student.

In the Gospels the twelve were usually called disciples because as long as Jesus was with them they were still learners.

B. APOSTLE—One sent forth; one chosen and sent with a special commission as the fully authorized representative of the sender.

Several things were true of the apostles:

1. They were chosen directly by the Lord Himself: Matthew 10:1; Mark 3:13; Luke 6:13.

2. They were endued with signs and gifts which were the divine credentials of their office: Matthew 10:1; Acts 28:7-9; Acts 5:12-16.

3. They had to be eyewitnesses of the resurrection: Acts 1:22; I Corinthians 9:1.

4. They will be judges over the twelve tribes during the kingdom:
Matthew 19:28.

Another definition that would be good to know:

C. APOSTOLIC AGE—The period in the history of the church when the apostles were alive. It begins with Pentecost and ends with the death of the last apostle, probably the Apostle John.

All the apostles were disciples, but not all disciples were apostles. The apostles were chosen from among the disciples (Luke 6:13). The office was not and could not be passed on to others.

II. WHO WERE THE APOSTLES?

Matthew 10:1-8; Mark 3:13-21; Luke 6:12-19; and Acts 1:13.

A. SIMON (whom Jesus named Peter).

B. ANDREW (Peter's brother).

C. JAMES (the son of Zebedee).

D. JOHN (the brother of James).

E. PHILIP.

F. BARTHOLOMEW.

G. THOMAS.

H. MATTHEW.

I. JAMES (the son of Alphaeus).

J. JUDAS (Also known as Lebbaeus and Thaddaeus—terms of endearment like our nicknames—Matt. 10:3; his real name was Judas—Luke 6:16).

K. SIMON (called Zelotes).

L. JUDAS ISCARIOT (who also was the traitor—Luke 6:16b).

Andrew

SCRIPTURE READING:
John 1:35-42; 6:1-14; 12:20-26

MEMORY VERSE: John 1:41:
> *"He first findeth his own brother Simon, and saith unto him, We have found the Messias, which is, being interpreted, the Christ."*

ANDREW: A Greek name meaning "manliness."

THE AIMS FOR THIS LESSON:
1. To help the student understand that God will and often does use ordinary people.
2. The importance of playing "second fiddle."
3. Practical lessons on soul winning.

I. ANDREW, THE SAINT

How many of you have ever heard the expression "Saint Andrew"? Who knows what a "saint" is? (Explain. See that the student understands the meaning of "saint.")A saint is not a super Christian, nor a Christian who has died and gone to be with the Lord; but every believer is a saint (II Thess. 1:10). Paul often addresses Christians as saints.

In John 1:35-40 Andrew had been listening to John the Baptist preach. John the Baptist said, "Behold the Lamb of God." He presented Jesus as God's sacrifice for sin; and, as a result,

Andrew trusted Christ. Andrew became a saint by believing on Jesus as God's sacrificial Lamb.

ILLUSTRATION:

A little boy was sitting in church with his mother on Sunday morning. He noticed the tall, stained-glass windows in which were images of people. He asked his mother, "Who are those people in the window?" She replied, "They are saints." "Oh," he said. "Now I know what a saint is; it's one who lets the light shine in."

II. ANDREW, THE SECOND FIDDLER

Make sure the student understands what a "second fiddler" is. He is the man behind the scenes.

A. ANDREW HAD A VERY POPULAR BROTHER WHOSE NAME WAS PETER.

Andrew was always referred to as Simon Peter's brother (John 6:8).

You will notice in the list of the apostles that Peter's name always appears first; but really it was Andrew who found Christ first; and then he brought his brother, Peter, to Christ (John 1:35-42).

Peter's name is found throughout the New Testament. He wrote epistles, preached sermons, and had over 3,000 converts on the day of Pentecost. On the other hand, Andrew is only mentioned three times in the Gospels.

B. PLAYING SECOND FIDDLE IS IMPORTANT.

Had it not been for Andrew behind the scenes, there might never have been an Apostle Peter.

ILLUSTRATION:

I know about Charles H. Spurgeon, the great preacher; but I don't know the name of the substitute preacher who was speaking the night Mr. Spurgeon visited the church and was saved.

C. SECOND FIDDLE DOES NOT MEAN A LOWER POSITION IN GOD'S SIGHT.

If God wants you to play second fiddle, then you would have to step down to play first fiddle.

D. IF GOD WANTS YOU TO PLAY SECOND FIDDLE, DO IT WELL. (DON'T GRUMBLE ABOUT IT.)

ILLUSTRATION:

A king had a beautiful garden with all kinds of plants, trees and flowers. One day while walking through the garden the king said to the pine tree, "Pine tree, why are you so sad today?" The pine tree answered, "Because I don't have large limbs like the big oak."

He walked by the big oak and said, "Big oak, why are you so sad today?" The oak replied, "Because I don't have shiny needles like the pine."

It seemed that all the trees and plants were unhappy because they were not just like another tree or plant—until he came to the daisy. The little daisy lifted up its head and smiled. And the king asked, "Little daisy, why are you so happy?" To which the little daisy replied, "Because when you put me here, I figured you wanted a little daisy just like me—so I am going to be the best daisy I can."

The instrument that needs to be played most in the church is second fiddle.

III. ANDREW, THE SOUL WINNER

Andrew is mentioned only three times in the Gospels, and each time he is bringing someone to Christ:

John 1 —Bringing his brother
John 6 —Bringing the little lad
John 12—Bringing the Greeks

A. HE WAS SURE OF HIS OWN SALVATION: John 1:41—"We *have* found the Messias."

There was alsolutely no doubt in Andrew's mind about

his salvation. No one can be a successful soul winner until he is sure of his own salvation.

B. HE WENT FIRST TO HIS LOVED ONES: John 1:41— "He *first* findeth his own brother."

C. HE WENT AFTER A DIFFICULT CASE.

Simon Peter was loud, outspoken, aggressive. Most people would have considered him a difficult case, but many times the difficult ones can be led to the Lord. And often they make great Christians.

D. HE BROUGHT PETER TO JESUS.

It is not enough to convert people to your denomination or to convert them to some particular doctrine. These things are well and good, but our chief aim should be to bring men to Christ.

E. HE WAS TACTFUL IN HIS APPROACH.

Since he had found the Saviour first, he could have said to his loud brother, "I have finally found Someone who can straighten you out." He could have taken the attitude, "I know something you don't know"; and for a second fiddler that would have been a real temptation.

F. HE WAS FRIENDLY.

When the hungry multitudes in John had nothing to eat, it was Andrew who said, "There is a lad here, which hath five barley loaves, and two small fishes"(John 6:9).

How did Andrew know about the lad? He had to get acquainted with him. You see, he had taken time to introduce himself to this little lad and to find out something about him. The lad had probably been impressed with Andrew's friendliness and had offered to share his lunch. (Prov. 18:24: "A man that hath friends must show himself friendly.") The successful soul winner first wins people to himself, then to Christ.

G. HE WAS A NEW CONVERT.

God expects all Christians to be witnesses, even new converts.

ILLUSTRATION:
When do you expect a candle to give out light—
when you first light it or after it burns halfway down?
God expects you to start letting your light shine the
moment you are saved.

Peter, the Man Who Fell but Rose Again

SCRIPTURE READING:
   Matthew 16:13-23; Luke 22:54-62; John 21

MEMORY VERSE: Matthew 16:16:
   "And Simon Peter answered and said, Thou art the Christ, the Son of the living God."

INTRODUCTION:
   Last week we studied about the Apostle Andrew, Simon Peter's brother. You will remember that it was Andrew who brought his brother to the Lord (John 1:30-42). One of the points we tried to make was that God can and often does use ordinary men, as in the case of Andrew.

   Today we study about Andrew's brother, Simon Peter; and we will see that God also uses extraordinary men.

BEFORE WE STUDY THIS LESSON, LET'S NOTICE SOME INTERESTING THINGS ABOUT THIS GREAT APOSTLE:
   1. His name always heads the list whether given in Matthew, Mark, Luke, or Acts, though he was not the first disciple.
   2. He always stands out as the spokesman for the twelve.
      It was Peter who asked, "How often shall my brother sin against me, and I forgive Him?" (Matt.18:21).
      It was Peter who inquired what was to be the reward of those who left all and followed Jesus (Matt. 19:27).

It was Peter who asked about the fig tree when it withered away (Mark 11:21).

It was Peter who answered, when Jesus asked the crowd, "Who touched me?" (Luke 8:45).

It was Peter who, just preceding Pentecost, suggested they elect another apostle to replace Judas.

It was Peter who preached on the day of Pentecost when 3,000 people were converted (Acts 2:14-41).

3. He was a married man (Mark 1:29-31); therefore, he could not have been the first pope as the Catholics claim.

4. His name was changed. His name was Simon, which means "hearing"; the Lord changed it to Peter, which means "rock." In the Gospel of John he is often called by both his old and new name, Simon Peter.

You will also notice that he was called Cephas. Cephas and Peter are the same names, both meaning "rock." Peter is the Greek name and Cephas is the Aramaic name. In the ancient world, almost everyone spoke the Greek language as well as his own language. That was the reason most people had two names: a Greek name by which he was known in his business and in the world, and then the name of his own native language by which he was known in private and to his friends.

I. PETER BELIEVING

Scripture: Matthew 16:13-23.

It doesn't matter who people in general think Jesus is, but who you or I believe He is makes the difference between Heaven or Hell (John 8:21, 24; Rom. 10:9).

Peter not only believed, but he also confessed. A public confession is important (Rom. 10:9-11).

Baptism is a means of public confession (Acts 2:41).

II. PETER BACKSLIDING

Scripture: Luke 22:54-62; John 21.

Make sure the students know what backsliding is. It is not the loss of salvation, but the loss of fellowship (I John 1:7-9).

A man does not backslide overnight; there is a gradual getting away from God. Dr. H.A. Ironside once said, "If you were ever closer to the Lord than you are now, then you are backslidden."

Notice the events that led to Peter's backsliding:

A. HE BECAME SELF-CONFIDENT: Mark 14:27-31; Luke 22:31-34.

> Stand up, stand up, for Jesus,
> Stand in His strength alone;
> The arm of *flesh* will fail you—
> Ye dare not trust your own.

B. HE FOLLOWED JESUS AFAR OFF: Luke 22:54.

This is often the trouble. We are afraid to be out and out for Jesus, afraid to be called fanatics.

Lenin once said, "I would rather have ten fanatics than ten thousand placid followers."

C. HE KEPT THE WRONG COMPANY: Luke 22:56.

Peter joined the enemy and warmed himself by the enemy's fire (I Cor. 15:33; Prov.13:20).

STORY: An old Scottish woman said, "Peter had nae [no] business among the flunkies."

STORY: A man had a parrot that got loose and flew out into the corn patch with the crows. An old farmer was shooting crows, and the parrot was wounded. The farmer went out to pick up the dead crows and saw the wounded parrot; he picked it up, and the parrot said, "A-a-ark, wrong crowd! Wrong crowd!"

D. HE DENIED CHRIST: Luke 22:57: ". . .I know him not."

E. HE CURSED AND SWORE: Mark 14:71.

F. HE LEFT THE MINISTRY: John 21:1-3: "I go a fishing."

This does not mean he was taking a fishing trip, but it

was his public announcement that he was leaving the ministry. He fully intended to quit forever.

G. HE INFLUENCED SIX OTHERS TO LEAVE THE MINISTRY AT THE SAME TIME: John 21:1-3— Thomas, Nathanael, the sons of Zebedee, and two other disciples.

III. PETER BEGINNING ANEW—HOW THE LORD BROUGHT PETER BACK

A. HE MADE HIM A BUSINESS FAILURE: "They toiled all night and caught nothing."

Remember that Peter was a very knowledgeable fisherman, and fishing was his occupation. If anybody could have caught fish, Peter could have; but he failed.

B. HE SHOWED PETER THAT IN CHRIST'S WILL HE COULD SUCCEED.

After obeying Christ and letting down the net at the Lord's command, they caught more than they could put in all the ships.

C. HE SHOWED HIS LOVING CONCERN AND HOW HE WOULD PROVIDE FOR HIS NEEDS BY PREPARING A WARM BREAKFAST OF BREAD AND FISH.

D. FINALLY, HE CUT DEEP INTO PETER'S OWN HEART AND ASKED, "DON'T YOU LOVE ME?"

CONCLUSION:

Two chapters later in the Bible, on the day of Pentecost, it was Peter who was anxious to preach. His sins were forgiven, and his fellowship had been restored. Now he was ready to preach again, and 3,000 souls were converted.

Philip, the Practical Apostle

SCRIPTURE READING:
John 1:43-46; 6:5-14; 12:20-22; 14:6-14

MEMORY VERSE: John 1:45:
"Philip findeth Nathanael, and saith unto him, We have found him, of whom Moses in the law, and the prophets, did write, Jesus of Nazareth, the son of Joseph."

INTRODUCTION:

So far in our studies of the apostles, we have studied Andrew and his brother, Simon Peter. Today we will study about one of their close friends, Philip, a man who lived in their city (John 1:44).

When we studied Andrew, we saw how God can and often does use ordinary men. In studying the Apostle Peter, we saw how God can and often does use extraordinary men. Today we will see that God uses very practical men. The one word that best describes Philip is "practical."

You will notice throughout the lesson how practical Philip was. Maybe you know someone who takes the attitude, "I won't believe anything that I cannot figure out or understand." In a sense, Philip was this sort of man.

(Share with your students some things they accept which they cannot understand, such as: electricity, television, etc.)

ILLUSTRATION:

Billy Sunday used to say, "I cannot understand how a chicken eats food, and it turns to feathers; a cat eats food, and it turns to fur; and a fish eats food, and it turns to scales."

He also said, "I cannot understand how a brown cow can eat green grass and give white milk, but I still enjoy drinking milk."

There are many things we accept that we do not understand.

I. PHILIP DESCRIBED

(Make the Apostle Philip real to your students. Talk about him in general and make him come alive to your class.)

A. PHILIP—A GREEK NAME MEANING "WARRIOR" OR "LOVER OF HORSES."

B. A CLOSE FRIEND OF ANDREW AND PETER; HE LIVED IN THE SAME FISHING VILLAGE WHERE THEY LIVED (John 1:44).

C. TIMID, RETIRING.

D. NOT TO BE CONFUSED WITH PHILIP THE DEACON.

One never reads of the Apostle Philip after Pentecost, and one never reads of Deacon Philip before the day of Pentecost.

E. THE ONE WORD THAT BEST DESCRIBES HIM IS "PRACTICAL."

II. PHILIP DECIDING

Scripture: John 1:43-46.

A. PHILIP WAS PROBABLY THAT OTHER DISCIPLE WHO WAS WITH ANDREW THE DAY THEY HEARD JOHN THE BAPTIST PREACHING OF "JESUS, THE LAMB OF GOD" (John 1).

B. JESUS FOUND PHILIP (John 1:43).

Andrew found his own brother, Simon Peter; but it was Jesus Himself who found Philip.

C. THE CALL TO "FAITH" AND THE CALL TO "FOLLOW" CAME AT ONCE (John 1:43).

Tradition says that Philip was the one who requested of Jesus that he might first go bury his father (Matt. 8:21,22).

D. PHILIP WAS NEVER READY TO TAKE A STEP FORWARD UNTIL HE WAS SURE OF HIS GROUND (John 1:45).

Philip had read all that Moses and the prophets had said about Christ; he wanted to be sure.

E. AS SOON AS PHILIP WAS SURE, HE SOUGHT TO BRING OTHERS TO CHRIST (John 1:45).

Contrast what Philip said to Nathanael with what Andrew said to Peter.

F. NATHANAEL SAID TO PHILIP, "CAN ANY GOOD THING COME OUT OF NAZARETH?" PRACTICAL PHILIP SAID, "COME AND SEE."

III. PHILIP TESTED

Scripture: John 6:5-14.

When the hungry multitudes had nothing to eat, Jesus asked Philip, "Whence shall we buy bread that these may eat?" Jesus knew how practical Philip was; and He wanted to see if Philip would act on faith or reason. After some figuring, Philip said, "Two hundred pennyworth is not sufficient for these that they may all take a little." But in multiplying the loaves and fishes, Jesus showed that one can be too practical. Philip looked at the multitudes and the money, when he should have looked at the master.

IV. PHILIP PRACTICAL TO THE END

In John 12, when the Greeks came to see Jesus, Philip's approach was the most practical. He knew that when the disciples were sent out, they were to go only to the lost sheep of Israel; and now the Gentiles wanted to see Jesus. What was the practical thing to do? He could not make up his mind, so he called Andrew.

In John 14, after being with Jesus three years and seeing the miracles that He performed, Philip was still not quite sure. He said, "Lord, show us the Father, and it sufficeth us." Jesus said, "Have I been so long time with you, and yet hast thou not known me?"

CONCLUSION:

The last mention of Philip is in Acts 1:13, just before Pentecost. Tradition says he did mission work in Asia Minor.

Nathanael

(or Bartholomew)

SCRIPTURE READING:
John 1:43-51

MEMORY VERSE: John 1:46:

*"And Nathanael said unto him, Can there any good thing
come out of Nazareth? Philip saith unto him, Come and
see."*

INTRODUCTION:

The only mention of Nathanael in the Scriptures other
than this passage in John 1 is the listing of the apostles
found in Matthew, Mark, Luke and Acts, except for a mention in John 21:2 in which he is said to be one of the disciples
who was with Peter when they went fishing.

I. THE MAN

A. HIS NAME.

Most scholars agree that Nathanael and Bartholomew
were one and the same. Bartholomew was probably
Nathanael's surname. Nathanael means "gift of God";
Bartholomew means "the son of Tolmai." He was,
therefore, Nathanael Bartholomew, or Nathanael, the son
of Tolmai.

Bartholomew and Philip are always paired together

because Philip brought Nathanael (or Bartholomew) to the Lord.

B. HE WAS GUILELESS: Scripture: John 1:47.

Nathanael was honest and open. He was not deceitful. Sometimes we feel that vile sinners need the Saviour; but we tend to think that the sincere, honest people are all right. But Nathanael needed the Lord just as much as did the maniac of Gadara.

All men are sinners, but all men do not manifest their sin natures in the same way.

C. HE WAS AN EARNEST SEEKER: Scripture: John 1:45:

"We have found him, of whom Moses in the law, and the prophets, did write, Jesus of Nazareth, the son of Joseph."

Philip implied by this statement that both he and Nathanael had been looking for Jesus. He also implied that Nathanael had been reading Moses and the Prophets—that is, the Old Testament.

D. HE WAS IGNORANT TO A POINT.

He knew about Moses and the prophets. He knew the Bible, but he did not know the Christ of the Bible.

ILLUSTRATION:

D.L. Moody said that the carpenters knew more about the ark than did Noah, but the carpenters were not saved from the flood.

ILLUSTRATION:

There was little distance between Nazareth and Galilee, but the news of Jesus had not traveled that distance. If it had been bad news, no doubt it would have traveled faster. People are more prone to tell bad news than they are to tell good news. Do your neighbors and friends and schoolmates know about Jesus?

E. HE WAS SOMEWHAT PREJUDICED.

He asked, "Can any good thing come out of Nazareth?"

His prejudice was not without basis; Philip's testimony was at fault.

1. Philip called him Jesus of Nazareth, a statement which really is not true. He was not a native of Nazareth, but of Bethlehem (Micah 5:2).

2. Philip called Him the son of Joseph. He was not the son of Joseph; He was the Son of God (John 3:16; 1:18).

Remember that Philip himself had just been saved, and he was eager to tell others about his new-found Saviour. He had much zeal, but little knowledge. He made a big blunder when witnessing to Nathanael, but Jesus used Philip in spite of his blunder. I am sure He has done the same thing for many poor, ignorant preachers. Once someone said that one of the proofs of the inspiration of the Bible is that it has stood under so much poor preaching.

Often people are prejudiced against Christianity due to the imperfections of Christians. We should so state the Gospel that if men be offended by it, it will be the Gospel which offends them, not our way of presenting it.

II. THE MASTER.

A. HE KNEW HE WAS A DESCENDANT OF JACOB: "Behold an Israelite indeed."

B. HE KNEW HIS CHARACTER: "In whom is no guile."
He knows about everyone of us, even the secret things that others do not know.

C. HE KNEW THINGS ABOUT NATHANAEL THAT NO ONE ELSE KNEW: "Before Philip called thee when thou wast under the fig tree, I saw thee."
I wonder what happened under that fig tree! Could it be a favorite prayer spot where Nathanael went to pray? Could it be a place where he had been making certain vows or a place of confession?
There are some hallowed spots in our lives that are almost too sacred to talk about. Before that preacher

spoke to you, Jesus saw you. He saw you when you were walking in the woods, when you were busy doing housework, when you were driving along the highway. Long before you were saved, He saw you.

STORY:

I felt definitely led of the Lord to make a visit one night. When I stopped in front of the house, I saw that the lights were off. I started not to stop, but somehow I felt I should. When I went and knocked, immediately a man opened the door. He had been standing there crying and praying that God would send someone along to show him how to be saved. Before he came to Christ, God had seen him under the fig tree.

III. THE MIRACLE.

A. NATHANAEL TRUSTED THE SAVIOUR AND WAS SAVED: "Nathanael answered and saith unto him, Rabbi, thou art the Son of God; thou art the King of Israel."

He confessed that Jesus was the Son of God. That is how every person is saved (Acts 8:36-38). The eunuch asked Philip, "See, here is water; what doth hinder me to be baptized?" And Philip said, "If thou believest with all thine heart, thou mayest." And he answered and said, "I believe that Jesus Christ is the Son of God. . ." and he baptized him.

B. JESUS TOLD HIM THAT HE WOULD SEE EVEN GREATER THINGS: John 1:50,51:

"Jesus answered and said unto him, Because I said unto thee, I saw thee under the fig tree, believest thou? thou shalt see greater things than these. And he saith unto him, Verily, verily, I say unto you, Hereafter ye shall see Heaven open, and the angels of God ascending and descending upon the Son of man."

It is wonderful to trust Christ as Saviour, but that is only the beginning. There are greater things to be seen, such as walking with the Saviour and learning more about

Him, studying the Bible and learning what we should do as Christians, and then willingly obeying it.

Paul speaks of being changed into the image of the Lord from one glorious experience to another: "But we all, with open face beholding as in a glass the glory of the Lord, are changed into the same image from glory to glory, even as by the Spirit of the Lord" (II Cor. 3:18).

CONCLUSION:

A. EVEN SINCERE, HONEST PEOPLE NEED TO KNOW THE SAVIOUR.

B. JESUS KNOWS ALL ABOUT US.

C. NATHANAEL OWED HIS FRIEND AN INTRODUCTION TO JESUS. HAVE YOU INTRODUCED OTHERS TO HIM?

D. WE ARE NOT TO STOP AT SALVATION. THERE ARE GREATER THINGS TO BE SEEN AND LEARNED. WALK IN THE LIGHT YOU HAVE BEEN GIVEN, AND YOU WILL RECEIVE MORE LIGHT.

E. NATHANAEL ACCEPTED THE CHALLENGE, "COME AND SEE." WILL YOU?

Matthew (Levi)

The Man Who Left All to Follow Christ

SCRIPTURE READING:
Matthew 9:1-13; Mark 2:13-17; Luke 5:27-32

MEMORY VERSE: Matthew 9:12:
"But when Jesus heard that, he said unto them, They that be whole need not a physician, but they that are sick."

INTRODUCTION:
Matthew was the son of Alphaeus. He had two names: Matthew, which means "the gift of Jehovah"; and Levi, which means "joined." He was joined to the world and to making money. Matthew was like many people in our society today. He measured success by wealth; and he was determined to make all the money he could no matter what it cost his fellow man, and even if he had to use questionable means to do it.

On our money we have written, "In God We Trust" when probably for many if would be more correct to say, "In *this* God we trust."

First Timothy 6:10—"For the love of money is the root of all evil. . . ." It is the root of all kinds of evil. (Amplified Version: "Through this craving some have been led astray.")

Whether the Lord changed Matthew's name when He called him, or whether Matthew changed his own name, we do not know.

There are four main points to this lesson: Matthew's Occupation, Matthew's Salvation, Matthew's Appreciation, and Matthew's Revelation.

I. MATTHEW'S OCCUPATION

A. HE WAS A PUBLICAN: Luke 5:27—"And after these things he went forth, and saw a publican, named Levi, sitting at the receipt of custom. . . ."

The word "publican" comes from the Latin word *publicannus*, which means "the collector of Roman revenue or taxes."

B. THERE WERE TWO CLASSES OF PUBLICANS:
   1. The chief of publicans (of which Zacchaeus was an example)—Luke 19:2.
   2. The ordinary publican (the lowest class of a servant engaged in the collection of revenue, of which Levi, or Matthew, was an example).

C. THE REWARD OF THE PUBLICAN WAS THAT HE COULD EXTORT FOR HIS OWN BENEFIT MORE THAN WAS OWED, AS LONG AS THE EXTORTION DID NOT LEAD TO REVOLT.

D. THEY WERE SPOKEN OF AS LEECHES AND WERE GENERALLY DISHONEST.

E. THEY BECAME RICH BY TAKING FROM THE PEOPLE.

F. THEY WERE REGARDED AS SUCH QUESTIONABLE PEOPLE THAT THEIR TESTIMONIES WERE NOT ALLOWED IN COURT.

G. IN THE NEW TESTAMENT THEY WERE REGARDED AS TRAITORS AND APOSTATES: THEY WERE CLASSIFIED WITH SINNERS, HARLOTS AND THE HEATHEN (Matt 9:11; 18:17; 21:31).

II. MATTHEW'S SALVATION

Matthew 9:9—"And as Jesus passed forth from thence, he saw a man, named Matthew, sitting at the receipt of custom: and he saith unto him, Follow me. And he arose, and followed him."

This is a little bit of autobiography. Matthew wrote this verse about himself. I can imagine that when he started writing this verse, he had to lay down his pen and wipe away the tears as he recalled his experience.

This is all he said about himself. He could not have said less. Humility is a true mark of conversion.

A. IT WAS A DISPLAY OF DIVINE POWER.

Notice where Matthew places the story of his conversion—immediately after the miracle of the healing of the palsied man, as if to say, "I'll tell you about a great miracle; then I'll tell you about an even greater miracle—about a dirty, old sinner being saved." When he arose to follow Christ, the only thing he took out of his old life was his pen and ink.

B. IT WAS A DISPLAY OF DIVINE KNOWLEDGE: Matthew 9:9—"And as Jesus passed forth from thence, he saw a man, named Matthew. . . ."

Notice that it does not say that Matthew saw Jesus, but Jesus saw him. In one glance Jesus could see through Matthew. He saw all that was in him. He saw what others could not see. He saw underlying motives. Nothing is hidden from the Lord. I believe Jesus saw more. I believe He saw what Matthew could be. He saw his nimble fingers entering in the books the money he had collected, and He could see Matthew writing the first book of the New Testament.

C. IT WAS A DISPLAY OF DIVINE GRACE.

Notice that Matthew was not engaged in praying when Jesus called him. He was not attending a church service when Jesus called him. He was not reading his Bible when Jesus called him. As a matter of fact, he was not even thinking about Jesus when Jesus called him. He was sitting at the receipt of custom engaged in a degrading business. What a display of divine grace (Eph. 2:8,9). The past makes no difference to Jesus. He saw the possibilities of the future.

D. IT WAS A DISPLAY OF THE SIMPLICITY OF SALVATION: Matthew 9:9—". . .And he arose, and followed him."

Jesus said, "He that believeth hath everlasting life." Some say, "I want this particular feeling." Others say, "I want such and such an experience." Others will not be satisfied without a vision. There is nothing simpler than salvation. Believe and be saved (John 3:18; 3:36; Acts 16:31). There *is* a difficult side to salvation; but, thank God, the difficulties have been taken care of by God Himself when He put His Son to death in our place.

E. IT WAS A DISPLAY OF HOPE FOR THE WORST OF SINNERS.

If Jesus would save Levi the publican, then there was hope for all the publicans, sinners, harlots, and even the heathen. There is no sinner so bad that Jesus cannot save him (Rom. 5:20).

STORY:

One day when George Whitefield was speaking, he made the statement: "Jesus will take the Devil's outcasts." After the service, he was invited to lunch with a well-to-do family. While having lunch, a member of the household said, "Mr. Whitefield, I disagree with something you said today." When Mr. Whitefield asked what it was with which he disagreed, he replied, "When you said, 'Jesus will take the Devil's outcasts. . . .' "

About that time a servant came with a note for Mr. Whitefield. It was from two women who were waiting at the door to see him. When Mr. Whitefield went to the door, the two sinful women were weeping and said, "Mr. Whitefield, we are the Devil's outcasts. Will Jesus really take us?" When Mr. Whitefield assured them that He would, then and there they both were saved. Of course, Mr. Whitefield then had no trouble convincing the man of the household of the truth of his statement.

III. MATTHEW'S APPRECIATION

Matthew gave a feast in his home for publicans and sinners and invited Jesus as the honored guest (Matt. 9:10-13).

1. The feast was a token of gratitude for his emancipation from a sordid occupation.
2. It was to commemorate his translation into a new life. Matthew wanted all to know that he was a new creation in Christ Jesus.
3. It was to declare his determination to follow and serve his new-found King.
4. It was his public confession of surrender to the call of Christ.
5. It was to introduce his old associates and friends to his new-found Saviour. There's never a man saved who wants to go to Heaven alone.

IV. MATTHEW'S REVELATION

The Bible is God's revelation to man. The book of Matthew is the revelation that God gave to the apostle. Revelation was the act of God revealing to the Bible writers the truths in the Bible. Inspiration was the act of God, the Holy Spirit, choosing from the writer's vocabulary words to perfectly match the truths He had already revealed so that the truth lost nothing when it was written down. Illumination is the act of the Holy Spirit enlightening us as we study the Word, giving us more light and more understanding.

CONCLUDING THOUGHTS:

A fifth-century church historian said that Matthew went to Ethiopia as a missionary and was martyred for his witness to the saving power of Jesus Christ.

Simon, the Zealous Apostles

SCRIPTURE READING:
Matthew 10:4; Mark 3:18; Luke 6:15; Acts 1:13

INTRODUCTION:

There are two Simons in the list of apostles: Simon called Peter, who is first on the list of the apostles; and Simon called Zelotes, who is eleventh on the list.

There is only one other apostle mentioned after Simon Zelotes, and that is Judas Iscariot.

It is interesting to notice that so little is said about some of the apostles when they are the men Jesus chose to fill this unique office. Practically nothing is said at all about Simon Zelotes. He is mentioned only four times in the passages of Scripture we have read. Nothing is said about him except that he is listed with the twelve apostles.

I. WHAT DO WE KNOW ABOUT HIM?

A. MATTHEW CALLED HIM SIMON THE CANAAN-ITE (Matt. 10:4).

B. MARK CALLS HIM SIMON THE CANAANITE (Mark 3:18).

C. LUKE REFERS TO HIM AS SIMON CALLED ZELOTES (Luke 6:15).

D. IN ACTS 1:13 HE IS CALLED SIMON ZELOTES.

That is all the Bible says about Simon.

The word "Canaanite" does not refer to his birthplace, but it is a word meaning "to be zealous."

The word "Zelotes" is a Greek word meaning the same as the word "Canaanite"—"to be zealous."

The one thing we know about Simon was that he was zealous.

II. WHERE DID HE GET THE NAME "ZELOTES"?

According to Josephus, there was a Jewish patriotic party founded about twenty years before the ministry of Jesus. This party was started in order to resist Roman aggression. They were known as Zealots. They resorted to violence in their hatred of the Romans, and this fanatical violence eventually provoked the Roman War of 70 A.D.

Zelotes was a nickname, and it identified Simon with their party. He was a member of the band of freedom fighters who believed in national freedom for Israel and who were extremely zealous for their country.

This was Simon before he became an apostle of Jesus Christ. Though he left the party, yet he became forever known as Simon the zealous.

III. WHY DID SIMON BECOME A DISCIPLE OF JESUS?

We cannot say for sure; but since he was a member of the Zealots and was so zealous for the national freedom of Israel, maybe he saw in Jesus one who could bring about this freedom from Rome. The disciples expected Jesus to restore again the kingdom to Israel (Acts 1:6).

IV. WHY DID JESUS CHOOSE SIMON AS AN APOSTLE?

Jesus knew Simon's feelings about the Roman government, and Jesus knew that he would soon teach, "Render unto Caesar the things which are Caesar's. . ." (Matt. 22:21). Still Jesus chose Simon. We do not know why; we can only speculate.

A. MAYBE JESUS CHOSE HIM BECAUSE HE SAW HE COULD CHANNEL HIS ZEAL.

B. IT COULD BE THAT SIMON HAD ZEAL WITHOUT KNOWLEDGE, AND JESUS PLANNED TO SUPPLY THE KNOWLEDGE (Romans 10:1-4).

C. IT COULD BE THAT JESUS WANTED VARIETY AND DIVERSITY IN THE GROUP OF APOSTLES.

How do you think Matthew and Simon got along? If you remember, Matthew was a tax-collector for the Roman government and, therefore, was looked down on by the other Jews. Simon was a member of the Zealots, a band of freedom fighters determined to overthrow the Roman government (II Cor. 5:17).

D. MAYBE JESUS WANTED SOME PEOPLE IN HIS GROUP WITH FANATICAL DEVOTION.

I remind you again of what Lenin said: "I would rather have ten fanatics than ten thousand placid followers."

Tradition says that Simon died by crucifixion, as did his Lord.

V. WHAT ARE SOME LESSONS WE CAN LEARN?

A. GOD WOULD HAVE EVERY CHRISTIAN TO BE ZEALOUS: Titus 2:14.

B. A PERSON'S ZEAL CAN WANE: Revelation 2:14; 3:19; Galatians 5:7.

Sometimes people get zealous about something new, but after awhile the zeal wanes.

C. ZEAL PROVOKES OTHERS TO DO GOOD: II Corinthians 9:2.

D. ZEAL CAN BE WRONGLY DIRECTED: Galatians 1:6; Acts 22:3,4: Galatians 1:14.

E. ZEAL SHOULD BE COUPLED WITH KNOWLEDGE: Romans 10:1-4.

STORY:

An airplane left Los Angeles for Hawaii. After a couple of hours, the zealous pilot announced, "I am sorry to inform you that we are lost. However, we are making good time."

STORY:

A man came speeding up the road in a bright red sports car and stopped to yell at a boy standing in his yard. "Hey, is the next town up this way?"

"Yes," the boy in the yard answered.

The man sped away. In a few minutes he was right back in front of the same house. "I thought you said the next town was up that way."

"It is, " the boy replied, "but I didn't say this road led to it."

Zeal without knowledge is like haste to a man in the dark.

John

SCRIPTURE READING:
Mark 9:38-41; 10:35-41; John 20:30,31; I John 4:11-21

MEMORY VERSE: I John 4:11:
"Beloved, if God so loved us, we ought also to love one another."

INTRODUCTION:

Last week we studied about Simon, the zealous apostle; and we saw that the Bible has very little to say about him; as a matter of fact, his name is mentioned only four times.

Today we will study about the Apostle John, and we find that the New Testament has much to say about him.

BEFORE WE STUDY THIS LESSON, LET'S NOTICE SOME INTERESTING THINGS ABOUT THIS GREAT APOSTLE:

1. He was the youngest of the apostles.

2. He was the son of Zebedee and brother of James (Matt. 4:21).

3. He was a fisherman (Matt. 4:21).

4. He was a member of the inner circle which consisted of Peter, James and John.

5. He was the disciple who sat next to Christ at the Last Supper (John 13:23).

6. He was the writer of five New Testament books:

The Gospel of John, I John, II John, III John, and Revelation.

In the Gospel of John, his name is not mentioned; but he refers to himself as "the disciple whom Jesus loved" (John 13:23; 21:20).

There are two main things we are going to study about the Apostle John:

1. The Traits of His Character.
2. The Theme of His Writing.

I. THE TRAITS OF HIS CHARACTER

A. EARLY LIFE.

In later life John became known as the loving apostle; but he was not always the tender, loving apostle that he became. Notice some bad character traits of his early life:

1. Intolerance (Mark 9:38-41).
2. Selfish Ambition (Mark 10:35-41).
3. Bad Temper (Luke 9:51-56; Mark 3:17).

B. LATER LIFE.

Now, notice some of the good character traits of John's later life:

1. Sympathy (John 19:26,27).
2. Faithfulness:
   John 19:25,26—
   He was with Jesus at the cross when all the others had fled.
   Revelation 1:9—
   "I, John, your brother and companion, sharer and participator with you in the tribulation and kingdom and patient endurance (which are) in Jesus Christ, was on the isle called Patmos, banished on account of my witnessing to the Word of God and the testimony, the proof, the evidence for Jesus Christ."—Amplified Version.

3. Love:
   First John 4:7-21—John is known as the apostle of love.

II. THE THEME OF HIS WRITING

A. BELIEVING.

When one reads the Gospel of John, he will notice that the key word is "believe." The word "believe" occurs 99 times in this Gospel.

The key verse of the book is John 20:31: "But these are written, that ye might believe that Jesus is the Christ, the Son of God; and that believing ye might have life through his name."

Make sure the students understand what it means to believe: to depend upon, to rely on, and to trust completely.

ILLUSTRATION:

A person believes in Jesus the same way he believes in a doctor. To believe in one's doctor is to have confidence in him that he is all he offers himself to be.

Jesus offers Himself to be your:

1. Sinbearer (Isa. 53:6; I Pet. 2:24).

2. Ransom (Mark 10:45).

3. Substitute (Rom. 5:8).

4. Atoning Sacrifice (I John 2:1,2).

B. LOVE ONE ANOTHER (I John 4:7-21).

There is a beautiful tradition of the last days of the Apostle John. He had gathered his friends for a parting message. As he looked into their faces with all tenderness, he said unto them, "Little children, love one another."

"But," they said, "we have heard that message before. You've been telling us that from the beginning. Give us some other word."

Looking down upon them with increased tenderness,

he said, "Little children, that which ye have heard from the beginning, that speak I unto you, that ye love one another."

Then his friends answered, "Ah, you have been giving us that message ever since we have known you. Soon you will be gone, and we want some parting word with which to remember you. Give us some new commandment tonight."

Then for the last time, John said, "Little children, dear little children, a new commandment I give unto you, that ye love one another."

He had no other commandment. All the commandments were bound up in this one. Love one another as Christ has loved you. Notice some things about this new Commandment:

1. The Longsuffering and Kindness of Love:
    First Corinthians 13:4a—"Love suffereth long, and is kind." (Love endures long and is patient—very patient. Love keeps on loving in spite of all neglect and abuse. Love is also kind.)

2. The Forgetfulness of Love:
    First Corinthians 13:5b—"Thinketh no evil." (That is, love does not take account of evil done to it.)

3. The Unselfishness of Love:
    First Corinthians 13:5—"Seeketh not her own." (Love does not insist on its own rights or its own way, for it is never self-seeking.)

4. The Coveringness of Love:
    First Corinthians 13:7—"Beareth all things." (Literally that means *covereth* all things.) "Believeth all things." (Love is always ready to believe the best of every person.)

5. The Practicalness of Love:
    First John 3:18—"My little children, let us not

love in word, neither in tongue; but in deed and in truth."

What does Jesus mean here? We usually think of love as an emotion. Love is actually doing, serving, helping, and ministering. The test of love is not the feeling of love in our hearts, but the deeds of love in our lives.

John 21:17—"Simon, lovest thou me?" Well, do something—"Feed my sheep."

God uses the thermometer of obedience to test the temperature of love. If you have become discouraged because your emotions fluctuate, remember that the final test of love is not how we feel, but how we live.

6. The All-Sufficiency of Love:

Romans 13:10b—"Love is the fulfilling of the law."

One cannot review all the commandments of the Bible at the end of every day and ask himself if he has kept everyone of them; he can, however, ask himself, has everything that I have done today been done in love?

Matthew 22:32-40.

James, the Brother of John

SCRIPTURE READING:
Matthew 4:21; 10:2; 20:20-28; Mark 1:16-20; 10:35-45; Luke 9:51-56; Acts 12:1,2

MEMORY VERSES: Acts 12:1,2:
"Now about that time Herod the king stretched forth his hands to vex certain of the church. And he killed James the brother of John with the sword."

JAMES: Means "supplanter"

INTRODUCTION:
Review briefly the Apostle John. James and John were brothers, and much that you will read today will be the same Scripture dealt with when we studied the Apostle John.

I. WHICH JAMES?

Ask the class if they can identify the three men who are referred to in the Gospels by this name.

The name James has probably caused more confusion than any other name in the New Testament because we read about two apostles and one other man by that name: James, the son of Zebedee; James, the son of Alphaeus; and James, the brother of our Lord.

A. THIS JAMES WAS THE SON OF ZEBEDEE: Matthew 4:21.

B. THIS JAMES WAS THE ELDER BROTHER OF THE APOSTLE JOHN: Matthew 4:21.

The reason I say that he was the elder brother is that his name is always mentioned first, which is an indication of an elder brother.

C. HE WAS A MEMBER OF THE INNER CIRCLE: Matthew 17:1; Mark 5:37; Mark 14:33.

D. HIS FATHER WAS A VERY PROSPEROUS GALILEAN FISHERMAN: Mark 1:20.

E. HE AND HIS BROTHER JOHN WORKED WITH THEIR FATHER: Mark 1:19.

F. HIS NAME IS ALWAYS COUPLED WITH HIS BROTHER JOHN.

They were evidently sent out as a pair.

They were of like spirit and disposition.

In Mark 3:17 Jesus calls them both "the sons of thunder."

G. THEY WERE PARTNERS WITH SIMON: Luke 5:10.

H. JAMES WAS THE SECOND CHRISTIAN MARTYR.

Stephen was the first Christian martyr (Acts 7).

James was the first apostle to be martyred (Acts 12).

There were seventeen years between his call to service and his death.

II. WHAT ABOUT HIS FAMILY?

A. JAMES WAS FROM A VERY PROSPEROUS FAMILY.

This is evidenced from the fact that his father employed servants to assist in the management of his boats (Mark 1:20).

B. HIS FATHER WAS A MAN OF SOCIAL POSITION.

He was known as a friend of the high priest, Caiaphas.

C. HE HAD A VERY AMBITIOUS MOTHER: Matthew 20:20-28.

His mother wanted her two sons, James and John, to

sit one on the right hand and one on the left in the
kingdom. She could not ask for two higher positions for
them.

Maybe she thought that Jesus was about to overthrow
the Roman government and establish His own kingdom,
and she was ambitious for her two sons, or maybe she
wasn't as ambitious for them as she was for herself.
Perhaps the only reason she wanted her two sons to oc-
cupy these high positions was her desire to be known as
the mother of James and John.

Sometimes parents try to fulfil ambitions through
their children. They want their children to be what they
could not be.

III. SO YOU WANT TO BE GREAT?

A. HIS MOTHER HAD ALREADY REQUESTED A
CHIEF POSITION FOR JAMES IN THE KINGDOM.

B. NOW JAMES HAS AMBITIONS OF HIS OWN. He
and John request to sit one on the right hand and one on
the left in the kingdom.

C. IT IS ALL RIGHT TO BE AMBITIOUS AS LONG AS
OUR AMBITIONS ARE NOT SELFISH.

They said not a word of concern for the ordeal the Lord
was facing at the hand of His enemies. "Just be sure you
give us the places nearest you."

Someone has said, "Aim high; it costs no more to shoot
at eagles than at skunks."

Every man is capable of being something better than
he is.

D. SOMETIMES A MAN'S AMBITIONS CAN BLIND
HIM: Mark 10:38,39.

I am not sure that James knew what he was talking
about when he said he was able to drink of the cup and
be baptized with the baptism with which Jesus was baptized.

He was so excited about achieving the position that he was blinded by his ambition.

E. DO YOU THINK JAMES WAS QUALIFIED FOR GREATNESS?

IV. *THE WAY TO GREATNESS:* Mark 10:43-45.

A loftier ambition than merely to stand high in the world is to stoop down and lift mankind a little higher.

STORY:

Bob Richards tells of John Landy who trained hard for two months in Australian championships. In Melbourne 50,000 people came out to watch John Landy—at that time one of the few sub-four minute milers—break his own world's record of 3:58.

Landy was running strongly by the end of the half. He smiled as he rounded the curve and heard the roar of the crowd. Running down the backstretch at a sensational pace, Landy saw a young high school runner stumble and fall. Without a moment's hesitation, John Landy stopped! He reached down, pulled the boy up, and waited to see that he was not hurt. The crowd was frantic! Then Landy went on to catch the other runners and came in at 4:04.2. The estimate by experts is: if Landy had not stopped, his time would have been 3:59 or under.

This is an unusual story. He was a man who was more concerned about a fallen runner than winning a national championship. One sportswriter commented that when the greatest sports stories are written, this runner will be remembered as the one more concerned about the people along the way than his achieving his own ambition.

V. *DID JAMES MAKE IT?*

A. JAMES BECAME THE SECOND CHRISTIAN MARTYR AND THE FIRST APOSTLE TO DIE FOR HIS FAITH: Acts 12:1,2.

B. JAMES HAD AN INTERESTING FINAL INFLU-
ENCE.

Secular history records a story that James' accuser was
so impressed by the apostle's faith in Christ—even under
torture—that he, too, believed in the Lord and, like
James, was beheaded for his faith.

Judas,
the Steadfast Apostle

SCRIPTURE READING:
John 14:16-26

MEMORY VERSE: John 14:23:
"Jesus answered and said unto him, If a man love me, he will keep my words: and my Father will love him, and we will come unto him, and make our abode with him."

I. WHO WAS JUDAS?

A. JUDAS WAS LISTED AMONG THE APOSTLES.

1. Matthew and Mark place Judas tenth in the list of the apostles.
2. In Luke and Acts, he is mentioned eleventh in the list.

B. DIFFERENT NAMES WERE GIVEN JUDAS.

1. Matthew calls him Lebbaeus whose surname was Thaddaeus.
2. Mark simply calls him Thaddaeus.
3. In Luke and Acts, he is called Judas.

His real name is Judas. Lebbaeus and Thaddaeus are terms of endearment, like our nicknames.

I do not know why Matthew and Mark did not use the name Judas instead of the nicknames Thaddaeus or Lebbaeus. It could be that after the crucifixion of Jesus, there was an awful stigma attached to the name of Judas because Judas Iscariot had sold the Lord for thirty pieces of silver.

C. THE NAME JUDAS MEANS "PRAISE."

D. HE WAS THE BROTHER OF JAMES: Luke 6:16; Acts 1:13.

E. THERE ARE TWO APOSTLES NAMED JUDAS: Luke 6:16:

"*Judas brother of James, and Judas Iscariot which also was the traitor.*"

F. THIS JUDAS IS NOT TO BE CONFUSED WITH JUDAS ISCARIOT.

The Bible is always careful to distinguish between the two: John 14:22; Luke 6:16.

II. *WHAT WAS THE OUTSTANDING QUALITY OF THIS APOSTLE?*

The Bible does not say much about the Apostle Judas. The only other mention of him, other than the list of the apostles, is in John 14:22.

The one word which comes to my mind concerning Judas is *STEADFASTNESS.*

"Stead" means a place or spot. For example, we say the homestead. "Fast" means firmly fixed in place. To be steadfast is to remain constant, to endure, to be firmly established, not to quit.

The steady person does not fade out of the picture. He is sturdy and fixed in purpose.

Why do I say Judas was the *STEADFAST APOSTLE?*

A. JUDAS DID NOT QUIT.

One Judas turned traitor, quit and sold Jesus to His enemies; but this Judas did not quit. He remained steadfast. Considering this trait is reason enough to call him the *STEADFAST APOSTLE.*

B. JUDAS INTENDED TO CONTINUE EVEN AFTER THE LORD HAD GONE BACK TO THE FATHER.

In John 14:16-26, Jesus is telling His disciples, "Yet a

little while, and the world seeth me no more." Then He goes on to tell them, "He that hath my commandments, and keepeth them, he it is that loveth me: and he that loveth me shall be loved of my Father, and I will love him, and will manifest myself to him."

And then Judas answered and said unto Him, "How is it that thou wilt manifest thyself unto us, and not unto the world?"

For at least three years, Judas had been steadily following our Lord. He had been faithful and dependable. Now Jesus implies some change, and Judas wants to make sure of what it will be. His question in John 14:22 indicates that he intends to be steadfast even after the Lord has gone back to the Father.

C. OUR LORD ENCOURAGED JUDAS TO BE STEADFAST· John 14:23—Keep on loving me and keep on doing my words; stay fixed in purpose; do not quit.

D. IT IS BELIEVED THAT JUDAS DIED A MARTYR'S DEATH IN PERSIA.
   He remained steadfast to the very end.

III. JESUS WOULD HAVE ALL HIS FOLLOWERS TO BE STEADFAST: I Corinthians 15:58; II Peter 3:17; Acts 2:42; I Peter 5:9.

What do you think is the most important quality for a Christian?

That he be talented? That he be spiritual? That he be steadfast?

I think the most important quality is to be *steadfast.*

What good is a twenty-piece orchestra composed of brilliant talent, if it is never known when they are going to arrive to play?

Dr. Bob Jones, Sr., said, "The best ability is dependability."

Dr. Lee Roberson said, "You may not be much, but you can be faithful."

OUR LORD WOULD HAVE US TO BE STEADFAST IN:

A. OUR LABORS FOR HIM: I Corinthians 15:58; Galatians 6:9.

STORY:

There is a marker on a rock near the top of Mount Washington, marking the spot where a woman climber lay down and died. She was so close to the top that she could almost hit it with a stone. A hundred steps more and she would have reached the shelter she sought, but she did not know this. Disheartened by the storm, beaten in body and distressed in spirit, she was at the end of her courage. She could not see a step ahead, so she lay down and died one hundred steps from her goal.

B. OUR RESISTANCE TO SATAN: I Peter 5:8,9.

We are never to give up the warfare but are to be consistent in our resistance to Satan. The word "resist" literally means to fight back.

STORY:

Napoleon was defeated at Waterloo in 1815 by Wellington. Wellington called his forces together and said, "Hard pounding this, gentlemen, but we will see who can pound the longest."

The victory seems to go to the one who can pound the longest.

STORY:

One of Andrew Jackson's boyhood friends said, "I could throw Andrew nine times out of ten, but he wouldn't stay thrown."

C. THE WORD OF GOD: Acts 2:42.

D. FELLOWSHIP: Acts 2:42.

E. PRAYERS: Acts 2:42.

F. WATCHFULNESS FOR HIS RETURN: Acts 1:10,11.

CONCLUDING THOUGHTS:

Two men may have the same name, the same environment,

the same friends; they may have sat under the same teaching and yet turn out differently.

Most of us cannot identify with Peter, James or John; but we can identify with Judas, the steadfast apostle.

Thomas

SCRIPTURE READING:
Matthew 10:3; Mark 3:18; Luke 6:15; John 11:1-16; 13:36-14:6; 20:19-29; Acts 1:13

MEMORY VERSE: John 20:29:
"Jesus saith unto him, Thomas, because thou hast seen me, thou hast believed: blessed are they that have not seen, and yet have believed."

AIM: To help the students see Thomas in a new light and understand that faith must have a basis.

INTRODUCTION:
Thomas, who is also called Didymus, has become known as "Doubting Thomas." Many words have been used to describe him—sullen, brooding, pessimistic, melancholy, etc.

Peter Marshall called him "the Palestinian Missourian."

I think it would be better to refer to him as "The Apostle Who Wanted to be Sure" rather than "Doubting Thomas." A careful study will reveal that he wanted a real basis for his faith.

There is no mention of him in the first three Gospels, except the mention of his name in the listing of the twelve. Had it not been for the Gospel of John, we would know nothing at all about him.

He is mentioned in the Gospel of John four times: In John 11 when Jesus raised Lazarus from the dead; in John 14 when Jesus talked about going to the Father; and in John 20 after the resurrection of Christ. He is also mentioned in John 21:2 as one of the disciples who went fishing with Peter.

Didymus is the Greek equivalent of Thomas, meaning Twin.

One of the reasons Thomas earned the title of "Doubting Thomas" is because he was so inquisitive.

Today, we are going to look at three incidents in the life of Thomas; and they will form the three-point outline.

I. *WHEN HE SAW WHAT HE OUGHT TO BELIEVE, HE ONLY WANTED TO KNOW THAT IT WAS RIGHT*: John 20:19-29.

    A. HE WANTED TO BELIEVE THAT JESUS HAD BEEN RAISED FROM THE DEAD, BUT HE WANTED TO BE SURE.

    B. HE WAS NOT WILLING TO BASE HIS FAITH ON THE TESTIMONY OF OTHERS; HE WANTED SOMETHING STRONGER.

    C. THERE IS NOTHING WRONG WITH WANTING A SURE BASIS FOR FAITH.

    D. THOMAS WOULD NOT MAKE A CONFESSION WITHOUT A THOROUGH INVESTIGATION.

        When Thomas exclaimed, "My Lord and my God," he believed with all his heart in the Lordship and Deity of Christ.

    E. FAITH IS BASED ON EVIDENCE OF THREE KINDS:

        1. Fact;

        2. Demonstrated performance;

        3. The witness of persons whose judgment and words one can trust.

    F. WHAT DOES JESUS WANT US TO BELIEVE TODAY? AND WHAT IS THE EVIDENCE ON WHICH WE BASE OUR FAITH?

        (Develop the three points.)

1. Fact—the fact of His resurrection.
2. Demonstrated performance—the change in thousands of sinners who have placed their faith in Christ.
3. The testimony of thousands of Christians.

G. ONCE THOMAS HAD A SURE BASIS FOR HIS FAITH, HE NEVER AGAIN DOUBTED THE RESURRECTION OF CHRIST.

II. *WHEN HE SAW WHAT HE OUGHT TO DO, HE ONLY WANTED TO KNOW HOW TO DO IT:* John 13:36-14:6.

A. I THANK GOD FOR THE INQUISITIVENESS AND HONESTY OF THOMAS.

Thomas said, "I don't know where you are going, and how can I know the way?"

Had Thomas not asked that question, we would never have had John 14:6—one of the most beautiful passages in the Bible.

B. JESUS HAD A THREEFOLD ANSWER.

It seems that Thomas asked only one question: "What is the way to the Father?" However, our Lord seems to have given answers: "I am the way, the truth, and the life."

C. WHAT DOES JESUS MEAN BY HIS ANSWER?

1. Christ is the way to all truth about the Father. No one knows the Father apart from Christ. All we know about God, we have learned through Jesus Christ (John 14:7).

   Christ teaches us the truth about:

   (a) God's love
   (b) God's mercy
   (c) God's justice
   (d) God's power

2. Christ meant that He was the way to life with the Father: I John 5:12.

   Men are dead in trespasses and sin, but they

become alive to the Father when they receive Christ.

3. Christ meant that He was the only way to go to Heaven and to be with the Father.

III. WHEN HE SAW WHAT HE OUGHT TO DO, NOTHING COULD KEEP HIM BACK: John 11:1-16.

Jesus' friend Lazarus had died.

After some time Jesus announced to the twelve that they would go back into Judea.

The disciples knew that the Jews of late had sought to stone Him, and questioned whether or not He should go (vs.8).

When Thomas saw that our Lord was going, he said, "Let us also go, that we may die with him" (vs.16).

Thomas' statement could be interpreted two ways. It was either a statement of deep devotion and determination, or it was the voice of a pessimist who saw only the bad side of everything. I believe it was a statement of deep devotion.

CONCLUSION:

Tradition says that Thomas went to India to preach and there became a martyr. Some traditions say that he was shot with arrows while praying.

The Malabar Christians of Saint Thomas in India still count Thomas as their first evangelist and martyr.

James, the Less

SCRIPTURE READING:
  Mark 6:3; 15:40; Luke 6:15,16; Galatians 1:19

MEMORY VERSE: James 2:18:
  *"Yea, a man may say, Thou hast faith, and I have works:
  shew me thy faith without thy works, and I will shew thee
  my faith by my works."*

I. *WHO IS HE?*
  A. THERE ARE TWO APOSTLES NAMED JAMES.
      We have studied about the other Apostle James, who
    was the brother of John and the son of Zebedee:
    Matthew 4:21.
      You will remember that he was the "ambitious
    apostle" who wanted to be great.
  B. THIS APOSTLE JAMES IS CALLED "JAMES THE
    LESS."
      James the Less—James the Little: Mark 15:40.
      He was probably called "James the less" because he
    was smaller in stature than the other James and was
    called "Little James" to distinguish him.
    ILLUSTRATION:
        When I was a little boy, I had an uncle named Pete
      and a first cousin who was also named Pete. When we
      were together, I would call my uncle "Pete" and my
      cousin "Little Pete," because he was smaller.
  C. SOME WRITERS BELIEVE THAT THERE WERE
    THREE MEN REFERRED TO IN THE BIBLE AS
    JAMES.
      1. James, the son of Zebedee, an apostle.

    2. James, the son of Alphaeus, another apostle.

    3. James, the brother of our Lord.

D. OTHER WRITERS BELIEVE THERE WERE ONLY TWO MEN IN THE NEW TESTAMENT NAMED JAMES.

    1. James, the son of Alphaeus.

    2. James, the son of Zebedee.

E. JAMES, THE SON OF ALPHAEUS, MAY BE JAMES, THE BROTHER OF OUR LORD.

    It is impossible to be absolutely sure; but it appears that James, the son of Alphaeus, and James, the brother of our Lord, are the same.

    1. Mark 15:40 states that James and Joses were brothers.

    2. Mark 6:3 states that Jesus was the brother of James, Joses, Juda and Simon.

    3. Galatians 1:19 states that that Apostle James was the Lord's brother; and since there were only two apostles named James, and the other was the brother of John, it appears that that apostle has to be the brother of our Lord.

F. THE WORD *"BROTHER"* or *"KINSMAN"* IS USED LOOSELY AND CAN MEAN COUSIN, ACCORDING TO JEWISH USAGE.

    James was the son of Alphaeus and Mary, the sister of our Lord's mother: Matthew 10:3; Mark 15:40.

    Thus, he was the *cousin* or, according to Jewish usage, *brother* of the Lord Jesus.

II. *WHAT DO WE KNOW ABOUT HIM?*

A. HE WAS A WITNESS OF CHRIST'S RESURRECTION: I Corinthians 15:7.

B. HE BECAME A PILLAR IN THE CHURCH AT JERUSALEM: Galatians 2:9,10; Acts 15:4-34; Matthew 4:21-Scofield notes.

C. HE WAS A MAN WHO BELIEVED IN THE POWER OF PRAYER.

    He devoted much space to prayer in his espistle.

    Because of his habit of always kneeling in intercession for the saints, his knees became calloused like a camel's—thus, he became known as "the man with camel's knees."

D. HE WAS THE WRITER OF THE EPISTLE WHICH BEARS HIS NAME.

1. The book of James teaches that we are justified before men by works.

   Explain that we are justified before God by faith (Rom. 5:1). Since faith is invisible, the only way we can be justified before men is by our works. Now talk about the necessity of works.

2. In chapters 1 and 2, he teaches we are justified before men by works. In chapters 3, 4, and 5 he teaches the way we are to justify ourselves before men.

   (a) In chapter 3, we are to justify ourselves before men by the way we talk.

   (b) In chapter 4, we are to justify ourselves before men by the way we live.

   (c) In chapter 5, we are to justify ourselves before men by the way we love and care for one another.

Judas Iscariot, the Betrayer

SCRIPTURE READING:
  Psalms 41:9; 109:5-8; Zechariah 11:12,13; Matthew 10:4; 26:14-50; 27:3-10; John 12:1-8; Acts 1:16-18

MEMORY VERSE: Psalm 109:6,7:
  "Set thou a wicked man over him: and let Satan stand at his right hand. When he shall be judged, let him be condemned: and let his prayer become sin."

INTRODUCTION:
  Judas Iscariot was one of the twelve chosen by the Lord Jesus to be with Him and to help Him in His earthly ministry. The surname Iscariot is usually understood to mean "man of Kerioth," (a city in the southern part of Judea). He was the only one from the south; the others were from the north. His father's name was Simon (John 13:2).

  When most people think of Judas, they think of a hard-looking criminal with a mean expression on his face; but as we study about him today, we will see that the other apostles had much confidence in him and there was no outward, obvious evidence of his being the kind of man who would betray Christ.

ILLUSTRATION:
  When I was a little boy, I remember seeing the painting of the Lord's Supper for the first time. I remember trying to pick out

Judas in the picture. I looked for the meanest one I could find. I just thought he had to look that way.

I. THE PROPHECY OF THE BETRAYAL.

A. JESUS WOULD BE BETRAYED BY A FRIEND:
   Prophesied in Psalm 41:9; Fulfilled in Matthew 26:50.

B. JESUS WOULD BE BETRAYED BY NOT ONLY A FRIEND BUT AN ASSOCIATE (A GUIDE):
   Prophesied in Psalm 55:12-14; Fulfilled in Acts 1:17.

C. THE OFFICE OF THE FRIEND AND GUIDE WOULD BE TAKEN AWAY:
   Prophesied in Psalm 109:8; Fulfilled in Acts 1:20.

D. THE PRICE OF A BASE SLAVE WAS FORETOLD:
   Prophesied in Zechariah 11:12,13; Fulfilled in Matthew 26:14,15.

How wonderful the Bible is! No honest person could doubt the inspiration of the Scripture when he sees the prophecy fulfilled.

II. THE POSITION AND REPUTATION OF THE BETRAYER.

A. JUDAS HELD A VERY HIGH POSITION AS ONE OF THE TWELVE. He was selected to be one of the twelve, not just one of the seventy.

B. JUDAS WAS A PREACHER: Acts 1:17.

C. JUDAS WAS THE TREASURER OF THE TWELVE: John 12:6.

D. ALL OF THE OTHER APOSTLES HAD CONFIDENCE IN JUDAS.
   They were willing to elect him treasurer; and even when Jesus said, "One of you shall betray me," they did not ask, "Is it Judas?" Rather, each asked, "Is it I?"

E. JUDAS WAS ALSO A MAN OF ABILITY, AS EVIDENCED BY HIS SERVING AS TREASURER.

F. HE HAD A PART IN THEIR MINISTRY: Acts 1:17.

G. HE SPENT THREE YEARS IN THE COMPANY OF JESUS.

H. HE WAS NOT THE HARD CRIMINAL THAT HE IS USUALLY THOUGHT TO BE.

He evidenced that he had a sensitive conscience. After he had committed the terrible sin, his conscience bothered him so much that he took the money back, then went out and hanged himself.

No position of honor or usefulness will guarantee our faithfulness or loyalty to Christ: Matthew 7:21,22.

The *worst* is the corruption of the *best*.

III. THE PICTURE OF THE CHARACTER OF THE BE-TRAYER

Dr. Bob Jones, Sr., said, "Your reputation is what people think you are; your character is what you are."

JUDAS HAD A GOOD REPUTATION BUT POOR CHARACTER.

One big thing stands out about Judas: he was covetous and greedy. He had ability to manage money, as was evidenced by his being elected treasurer; but that was the very area in which Satan tempted him.

First Timothy 6:10: "The love of money is the root of all evil."

Not getting money. . .not keeping money. . .but loving money.

There is nothing wrong with getting money, but it is bad to love it.

Judas was so anxious for gain that he did not even put a price on the Saviour, but asked the chief priest, "What will you give me?"

An old Puritan said, "That's not the way people usually trade. They generally tell their own price, but Judas was willing to sell the Lord of Glory at the buyer's price."

He could have been paid more for the Saviour, but

he was willing to sell Him for thirty pieces of silver—
the price of a base slave.

The chief priest did not come to Judas—Judas went
to him.

No one becomes a traitor all at once. Judas had been
stealing a little from the treasury all along, and now he
was willing to sell his Lord for gain: John 12:6.

IV. THE PATIENCE OF THE BETRAYED

In studying about Judas, it is important to notice the
wonderful patience of the Saviour.

A. JESUS WASHED THE FEET OF JUDAS AND THE
OTHER DISCIPLES THE DAY BEFORE HIS
BETRAYAL, KNOWING THAT JUDAS WOULD
BETRAY HIM: John 13:10,11.

B. AT THE TABLE JESUS KNEW THAT JUDAS
WOULD BETRAY HIM: John 13:21.

C. JESUS CALLED JUDAS "FRIEND" EVEN AFTER
JUDAS HAD BARGAINED WITH THE ENEMY AND
HAD COME TO BETRAY JESUS: Matthew 26:50.

V. THE POSSIBILITY OF THE FUTURE OF THE BETRAYER

A. THE BIBLE SEEMS TO INDICATE THAT JUDAS
WAS THE DEVIL INCARNATE AS JESUS WAS GOD
INCARNATE: John 6:70; 13:27.

B. JESUS CALLED JUDAS THE "SON OF PER-
DITION": John 17:12.

The beast is said to "go into perdition" (Rev. 17:8,11).

C. THE BIBLE SAYS, "HE WENT TO HIS OWN
PLACE": Matthew 25:41; Acts 1:25.

CONCLUDING THOUGHTS:

1. The journey into sin gains momentum. We never know
where a wrong path may end, or when one little sin may
lead to Satan's getting his foot in the door.

2. There will be times when you will have to face the decision: Christ or thirty pieces of silver?

You will have an opportunity to make more, but it will mean your sacrificing Christian convictions.

You will have an opportunity to be popular, but it will mean sacrificing Christian convictions.

You will have an opportunity to get ahead in life, but you will have to sacrifice your Christian convictions.

WHATEVER YOU DO, DON'T BETRAY HIM!